Musical Families

The String Family in Harmony!

by Trisha Speed Shaskan

illustrated by Robert Meganck

PICTURE WINDOW BOOKS
a capstone imprint

Special thanks to our advisers for their expertise:

Rick Orpen, PhD, Professor of Music, Gustavus Adolphus College
Terry Flaherty, PhD, Professor of English, Minnesota State University, Mankato

Picture Window Books
151 Good Counsel Drive
P.O. Box 669
Mankato, MN 56002-0669
877-845-8392
www.capstonepub.com

Editor: Jill Kalz
Designer: Lori Bye
Art Director: Nathan Gassman
Production Specialist: Jane Klenk
The illustrations in this book were
created digitally.

Printed in the United States of America in North Mankato, Minnesota
032010
005740CGF10

All books published by Picture Window Books
are manufactured with paper containing at least
10 percent post-consumer waste.

Library of Congress Cataloging-in-Publication Data
Shaskan, Trisha Speed, 1973–
The string family in harmony! / by Trisha Speed Shaskan ; illustrated
by Robert Meganck.
p. cm. — (Musical families)
Includes index.
ISBN 978-1-4048-6043-8 (library binding)
1. Stringed instruments—Juvenile literature. I. Meganck, Robert. II.
Title.
ML750.S53 2011
787'.19—dc22
2010001095

Each member of my family is a different size. We each make our own sound. But one thing brings us together—strings!

We're called string instruments because our sounds come from our strings. A musician makes the strings vibrate with his fingers or a bow. When the strings vibrate, we make music.

TWANG!

ZING! ZING!

More than 1,500 years ago, instrument strings in the Middle East were made of gold. Today strings are made of animal gut, steel, or nylon.

Harlo has his own style. Harps are shaped like triangles.

The rest of us look more alike. Guitars, violins, violas, cellos, and double basses have a hollow wooden body and a long neck. Our strings are stretched from our pegs to our tailpiece.

peg

neck

tailpiece

7

Everyone in my family is an artist. My dad, like all violins, uses every color there is, from the

prettiest pink

to the

grumpiest gray.

To play a violin, some musicians hold it under their chin. Others hold it against their chest. A few even rest it against their jaw.

The two S-shaped holes in the body of a violin, viola, cello, and double bass are called F-holes. These holes make the instruments sound louder.

Mom and Dad have the same shape and are played the same way. But they don't sound exactly alike. Mom makes a lower, fuller sound. Her music feels warmer.

Violas are a little bigger than violins. They have longer, thicker strings. And they're played with a heavier bow.

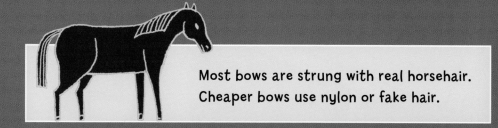

Most bows are strung with real horsehair. Cheaper bows use nylon or fake hair.

I play even lower notes than my mom and dad. Cellos can sound a **little gloomy** sometimes. But we're still great artists!

12

A cello is too big to tuck under a musician's chin. Instead, it stands upright and rests between a musician's knees.

A cello stands on a metal peg called a tail spike or end pin. So does a double bass.

My sister Casey is the biggest instrument played with a bow. She's also the lowest-sounding stringed instrument in the orchestra. Her music rumbles inside a listener's bones.

A double bass adds rhythm. It holds all the other instruments' sounds together like glue.

A double bass is also called a string bass, upright bass, bass viol, or bass.

My brother, Harlo, is usually a quiet, cool guy. But he can be **jazzy** and filled with **fire** too!

To play a harp, a musician plucks the strings. Foot pedals help change the sound.

A pedal harp has seven foot pedals and 47 strings.

Even Gitsy, the guitar of the family, is an artist. She likes to harmonize.

If I sound **sad**, she'll sound **excited**.
And **together** we'll sound **happy**!

That's how harmony works. It takes yellow and blue to make green. And it takes more than one note to harmonize.

Yes! Harmony!

22

Glossary

bow—a rod strung with horsehair used to play most string instruments

harmonize—to group together in a pleasing way; *harmony* is the result

musician—a person who plays music

orchestra—a group of musicians who play together on various instruments, especially violins and other string instruments

pluck—to pull at and then let go of

rhythm—a pattern of beats

vibrate—to move back and forth very quickly

Fun Facts

There are usually more violins in an orchestra than any other instrument.

Before the 1800s, women didn't play the cello. The playing position was thought to be too unladylike.

The first guitar was called a gittern. It was small and had only four strings.

A pedal harp stands about 6 feet (1.8 meters) tall and weighs about 90 pounds (41 kilograms). Pedal harps are also called concert harps, grand harps, or orchestral harps.

To Learn More

More Books to Read

Aliki. *Ah, Music!* New York: HarperCollins, 2003.

Helsby, Genevieve, with Marin Alsop. *Those Amazing Musical Instruments.* Naperville, Ill.: Sourcebooks, 2007.

Storey, Rita. *The Violin and Other Stringed Instruments.* Let's Make Music. Mankato, Minn.: Smart Apple Media, 2010.

Internet Sites

FactHound offers a safe, fun way to find Internet sites related to this book.

All of the sites on FactHound have been researched by our staff.

Here's all you do:

Visit *www.facthound.com*

FactHound will fetch the best sites for you!

Index

Look for all the books in the Musical Families series:

Around the World with the Percussion Family!

The Brass Family on Parade!

The Keyboard Family Takes Center Stage!

Opening Night with the Woodwind Family!

The String Family in Harmony!